MW00607984

My Childrens

Adela Najarro

Published by Unsolicited Press.
All Rights Reserved.
Copyright© 2017. Adela Najarro
This work was made possible in collaboration with the Puente
Project. We want to thank them for their dedication to poetry and
Adela Najarro for her keen perspective on the world.

Books may be purchased directly from the publisher or major
retailers. Also available via Ingram.

ISBN: 978-0-9980872-8-3

Contents

Preface

 It is difficult
to get the news from poems
         yet men die miserably every day
                  for lack
of what is found there.
                  --- William Carlos Williams "Asphodel, That
Greeny Flower"

Williams' lines bring to mind how important poems can be, not
because poems will improve test scores or create job skills, but
because poems address the spirit, that deep down part ourselves
that we live with every day. It is that inner self to which poems
speak. Looking at Williams' lines about death, it's not just the
physical body that can die miserably but the spirit too. The spirit
dies when hope, love, joy, wonder are absent; these life affirming
emotions reside in poems. Students can even find a version of
their own truth in a poem.

Poetry is about what matters deep down inside. The poems collected in this book all focus on the US Latinx experience through the voice of my own background as a child born in the US to Nicaraguan immigrants. It might seem a stretch to share poems by a Nica with Mexican-American students or students from a wide range of homelands, but we share language, culture, and an immigration history. All Latin American nations and those in the Caribbean have in common the Spanish conquest and a complex and troubled relationship with the United States. From this history arise questions concerning identity and culture. Are we Americans, Mexicans, Nicaraguans, Salvadorans, Puertoriqueños or Puerto Ricans? What does it mean to live in the United States knowing that your family had nothing to do with pilgrims or covered wagons? Which language should we speak, Spanish, English, or Spanglish? Isn't speaking Spanglish wrong and incorrect?

The selected poems in this volume raise questions about what it means to live in the US as a person of color, as a Hispanic person, as a Latinx. There are no set answers and we all travel the path of identity formation over and over. I have come to identify as a US Latina since the Latinx story of US history has always included Spanish, the Caribbean, and the Americas. These Latinx poems are US American poems and are relevant to all races and ethnicities since they voice concerns about the largest ethnic enclave in the US—Latinx, Latinos, Hispanics, and all the other terms by which we are named. I hope that by reading these poems, questions will arise about identity and what it means to be American. The purpose is to question, think, and then perhaps write back in response.

How to Use This Book

I was thrilled the first time that I read a Latinx book and encountered characters that looked like me and who spoke Spanglish. It felt natural. There was no need to question what things were or to look up every other word in a dictionary. I was caught in the literary flow. Finally, the words were meant for me. When we read, we expand our knowledge of the world, and when we include the Latinx experience in a course, students relate to their own situations or learn about things they may not have thought of. It is so important for everyone to visualize themselves in the books they read. Thank you for sharing these poems with your classes.

There are many ways to use this collection, and what follows is a brief survey of possible classroom uses:

1. **Assign an essay:** specific themes reoccur throughout the volume which lend themselves to a literary analysis essay or a research project. (These themes are outlined in the following section.)
   a. The entire collection could be assigned and students present a close reading of three poems on a theme they identify.
   b. Students complete a close reading of several poems followed by an analysis of how these themes exist in their own lives—basically they analyze the poems and then explain how similar situations occur in their own lives.
   c. Students research one theme and include the collection as one source. For example, students could research Spanglish, immigration, or education, then analyze a poem that fits the theme as a source for their research project. (This type of essay would

include mostly non-fiction articles with a close reading of a poem as an additional source.)

2. **Reader responses:** assign poems as homework and have students write their response. When assigning reader responses, I have students choose from the following:

   a. Summarize the poem. What are the main points of the reading? What happens at the beginning, the middle, and the end? What do you think the poem is about?

   b. Translate what the author is saying into your own words. What is the main point of the text? What is the overall meaning of the poem? What is the poem saying line by line or stanza by stanza?

   c. Connect the reading to your own personal experience. Does the poem remind you of something in your own life?

   d. Argue with the poem. Do you agree or disagree? What do you think should happen?

   e. Evaluate the poem. Would you recommend this poem to others? Why or why not?

   f. Choose a provocative sentence or line in the poem and write your response. What does this sentence or line make you think about?

3. **Creative Writing Journals:** use the supplemental pages and have students write in response to the writing prompt.

   a. After discussing poems in class, students can write their own poems following the writing prompt in the comment sections.

   b. Students can respond to one, some, or all of the writing prompts to make a creative writing portfolio or their own book.

   c. The writing prompts can be responded to in poetry or prose. Have students respond in both ways to the same prompt and then discuss the similarities and differences between poetry and prose.

4. **In-Class Discussion:** discuss the poem, the poem comment, and the questions that appear on the supplemental pages.

a. Assign small groups different poems and identify themes.
b. Assign half of the class the poem and the other half the comment on the poem. Hold a discussion on the themes presented.
c. Open class by reading one poem, then have students answer questions from the supplemental pages.
d. End class by reading one poem as a way to leave them thinking.

5. **Miscellaneous but necessary ideas!** There are many ways to allow poetry into the classroom and to inspire creative projects.
   a. **Illustrate**: have students choose one poem and illustrate the poem. They can also write the poem on their illustration.
   b. **Make a Poster:** students can choose a theme and then design a poster illustrating that theme with quotes from the poems and pictures they find in magazines or other sources.
   c. **PowerPoint Presentation:** In small groups or individually, students can present their analysis of a poem, theme, or the entire collection as a PowerPoint.
   d. **Video:** Students can perform a poem and then post to Youtube.
   e. **Recording:** Students can record a poem and place on a classroom or school website.

Thematic Guide to the Contents

As a poet, educator and scholar, I know that my own work isn't just about me. The poems in the collection reflect the US Latinx experience, and the themes present in the poems are relevant to all peoples in the United States. In addition, the poems present an opportunity to discuss our lives and culture while considering the perspective of immigrants and people of color.

Each theme listed below also notes which poems fit these broad categories. By starting discussion based on a theme, this approach can be used to pull in all the diverse voices in your classroom.

Family Relationships: these poems can spark discussions about what a family entails; why are we so attached to our families; how are families similar and different among different ethnicities and nationalities; is there something in common for all families?

Imaging the Homeland: immigrant populations in the United States remain tied to the homeland through story, emotion, and the past. The following poems can spark discussions about immigration, the costs and benefits of leaving the homeland, the costs and benefits of living in the United States, and how the past influences the present.

San Martín de Porres
An Ambiguity
Red Ants, Black Ants
Early Morning Chat with God
San Francisco
Conversation with Rubén Darío's "Eco y yo"
Lorca's Rain

Language: The United States has always been a multi-lingual nation. The following poems all contain Spanish within English as a way to show that Spanglish is a linguistic variant of the US Latinx population. The following poems can spark discussions about language and if there truly is a "right" way to speak, write, and think; what are the costs and benefits of being bilingual; how does it feel to read Spanglish; what languages are part of the US landscape?

San Martín de Porres
An Ambiguity
Chicanos in a Museum
San Francisco
Conversation with Rubén Darío's "Eco y yo"
Idiomas Desconocidas
Lorca's Rain

Education: the following poems relate to education in many forms; in many Latin American nations education comes with a prohibitive cost, so what happens to the children? Also, here in the States what do we learn about being Latinx or a person of color in school, in museums, in our culture at large? If education is something all should value, then what are we learning?

Religion: since the conquest, Latin America has been culturally influenced by the Catholic Church. The following poems can open a discussion about the historic effects of Catholicism on the Latinx imagination and life.

Race, Culture, and Identity: if we jump into the melting pot, we burn. Instead, acceptance of race and ethnic cultures should be viewed as a positive aspect of one's identity. The following poems address the difficulties found being Latinx in the United States. What are the perils and pitfalls for a person of color in the United States? Is there a way to correlate and combine contradictions between race, ethnicity and living in the United States? Who are we and who should we be? How does race and culture fit into identity?

Gender: another fluid aspect of identity is gender and how we interpret those parameters. The following poems can lead to discussions about gender roles; how do gender roles differ between nations; what does it mean to be Latina; what contributions do women make to our lives, to culture, and to history?

    An Ambiguity
    Una Muchachita
    Mujeres

San Martín de Porres

I found my grandmother in a shoe box
and through a mirror. She is the center of a corn tortilla
layered with leftover chicken and Monterey jack cheese.
Us cousins, los primos, are folded under
a rosary and Abuelita Aminta's santos.
Nuestra familia at the feet of the saints
in her bedroom altar, when I was plump
as an Iowa corn fed chicken
in California, Pico Rivera, and my mother
exalted my meaty legs,
hers were thin to the bone.

As a teenager, with a new beginning
of voluptuous curves,
I spent four weeks in Nicaragua
for a quick look around at the homeland. A storm
came in and the sky

slid black. Overgrown trees, bushes,
an entire wall of green lining a paved asphalt highway,
reached up, electrified,
as though all was alive, in need
of water, of rain, in need of a storm,
la tormenta. A word

that holds within itself the tumultuous sky, how nature,
my nature, our nature

is the cause of suffering, and how an angry downpour
is always ready and willing to wipe us clean.
El clima es bárbaro.
The climate will kill you with its gentle murmurs
and violent caresses.

Nicaragua's heat and humidity. Moist air
alive in itself. I have kept moving north and dream
of snow, quiet,
cool clear ice. I want it cold
and gray, snow angels fanned under three pine trees.

Place a finger on an ice cube and it melts back
to water, back to the essential,
back to the love of nuestra familia.
Before anger,

I sketched Abuelita Aminta
in a college-ruled notebook, and found
a Snicker's bar on a curio shelf. In my mouth
melted sugary sweet chocolate as I
ventured into her bedroom.
There Abuelita had propped my picture
up against San Martín de Porres, a Dominican
Brother found suspended in air
over a church floor, ecstatic in prayer for the lost,
for the homeless and the homebound.

Comment on "San Martín de Porres"

In my family, we never hired babysitters. Instead we would spend time with our tías, tíos, primos, and most importantly, our abuelitas. My Abuelita 'Minta would take care of me all the time during elementary school. My mom would drop me off, and then hours later pick me up. Abuelita 'Minta made the best quesadillas with lots of gooey Monterrey Jack cheese. The poem "San Martín de Porres" contains some of my favorite memories. Once, I snuck into my grandma's bedroom looking for candy and found my third grade picture at the foot of a statue of San Martín de Porres. In this poem, I explore the love I have for my family and try to wrap it up into a discovery of who I am and what is important in life.

Poetry is discovery. As a writer, sometimes we discover what is important to ourselves, our culture, even humanity in general. When I write, I'm on a journey poking around memories and looking into the past while thinking about who I am now. These memories, ideas, even stories, are placed into words, language, and in doing so a little bit of magic happens; that's how a poem ends up on a page. Reading a poem is also a journey of discovery. So much can be found in a poem. Discover where words can take you by reading a poem, but don't stop there. Read, and then read again. By reading a poem multiple times, you'll find out how much there is contained within the words and language that relate the stories of our lives.

1.   What discovery does the speaker of the poem make by the poem's end?
2.   How does the speaker of the poem feel about her family?
3.   What connections can you make between your family and the family in this poem?
4.   Have you ever travelled to another country?
5.   What does the speaker of the poem learn about Nicaragua?

Writing Prompt

Think about one of your grandmothers, or an elderly woman who is important to you. If you were going to find her, where would she be? At home? In a closet? In the kitchen? In Mexico? Describe where you can find your grandmother and what she would be doing. Make sure to use a metaphor: My grandmother is X. Is she a corn tortilla, like in the poem, or is she a tiger, lion, eagle? Write about your grandmother and explore the metaphor.

Look it Up!

1.   Where is the country of Nicaragua?
2.   What is the typical climate of Nicaragua?
3.   Who is San Martín de Porres?

An Ambiguity

Until syllables undulate a Nicaraguan cadence,
I am a white girl. Once I was asked,

"Where'd the green eyes come from?"
The question arising from longing for a simple

explanation: a gringo father and a love story
where Lupita throws down a rose. Un amorcito

mío once told me not to worry because I was
brown inside. Even so, for a while I dyed my hair

almost black. I still wear gold hoop earrings,
but I haven't tattooed that iguana on the inside

of my right wrist. Her Honorableness Sotomayor
got rid of the subdued hues and laid on

red nail polish after her confirmation. She began
the business of being herself. My mother

keeps insisting that I was born blond. Blondness.
Whiteness. I have been so confused.

I look in the mirror y quiero un color quemado.
A burnt umber. La pimienta. The prickly spice

of tropical brown. But I am güera, chele, fair skinned,
blanquita. Desde América Latina.

Latin America. The history.
My eyes from los conquistadores.

From genocide. From collision

and a struggle

to survive.

Comment on "An Ambiguity"

My family is mixed like all families in Latin America. My
mother's side of the family are fair skinned, while my father's
side of the family are various shades of brown. Mix them
together and we have a rainbow! In Mexico, being fair-skinned is
referred to as güero, while in Nicaragua, the term used is chele.
My family would always mention my skin color: ¡Eres una
chelita! I couldn't help but notice since everyone was telling me
about it, all the time. Everyone pretends that skin color doesn't
matter, but we all know that it does. Think about it. What color is
an American? What about someone from Mexico? We know that
people come in all colors, but in general we think of Americans
as white and Latinos as brown. Even though that's not true!

Being from Nicaraguan heritage while living in California made me want to be a Chicana, and Chicanas are supposed to be brown. What I found out was: ¡Soy Chicana porque me da la gana! We are more complex than skin color, but I had to think about where all this fuss over skin color started. I went back to the beginning. When Europeans left their continent, they took with them a powerful weapon: the idea that whiteness was better than any other skin color. The idea of white superiority has infected the world, and I had to look at my own skin color through this knowledge. If I was a mixture, and I looked white, then that meant my genes were a result of the conquest, of Spanish soldiers landing in the Americas and conceiving children with indigenous women. Somewhere past in time, somewhere along my family tree, European and indigenous genes mixed—I don't know the exact how or when. I can only imagine that survival was at stake.

Questions

1.   How do you imagine the speaker of the poem? What does she want to look like?

2.   Why does the Honorable Sotomayor wait until after confirmation as a Supreme Court Justice of the United States to wear red finger nail polish?

3.   What connections can you make between your own history and that described in the poem?

4.   What does genocide refer to in the poem?

5.   How does the poem begin and end? Describe how the mood and tone changes.

Writing Prompt

Let's do the hard work. We all know what color we are. We might wish to live in a colorblind world, but that's not reality. Write about what color you are. Include at least three different ways to name your skin color and at least two memories about comments on how you look. Are you comfortable with how you look? Are you uncomfortable? Have you received positive or negative messages about your skin color? What does your family believe about skin color? What do you believe? How is skin color part of who you are?

Look it Up!

1.   Did you know that whiteness is more than a color? It's an entire field of academic study: Whiteness Studies. Look it up. (Articles by Dr. Gregory Jay, Professor of English University of Wisconsin, Milwaukee, offer excellent information on this topic.)

2.   The Conquest. Why and when did Europeans leave Europe and conquer all indigenous people living in what is now known as the Americas?

3.   What is Latin America? How many countries? How are the countries in Latin America similar and different?

Una Muchachita

You see it's me I saw on a signpost in Watsonville. El corazón
es rojo y suda lágrimas. Luuuucky. The name of my cat.
Black and white with a heart. La flor. El caracol.

La puerta estaba abierta. I looked upon the sun and wondered...
Big bright yellow thing in the sky. Sol
is sun. One word for something so big. The language in me.

"Is not enuf for yu?" No. No. I'm a little girl. Una muchachita.
Take it like a man! An American! Stand up.
Sit down. Fight. Fight. Fight. But I don't talk like you.

I don't think like you. That means I don't know nothing. ¿Sí?
See? Which language? Yes? If I can catch the words
will you give me a job as a singer in a band? A marching band

on the Fourth of July. Red, white and blue are the colors that
stand
for you. But me rhymes with flea. La cucaracha ya no pudo
caminar.
He got caught and was squashed by a Texan's steel toe boot.

Comment on "Una Muchachita"

My first language was Spanish, but I learned English in pre-school. I've been able to figure out that I have been bilingual since the age of three or so. Even though I learned Spanish first, English is also "my" language. I've been mixing Spanish and English my whole life, so my native language must be Spanglish! Over the years I've come to realize that as a Latina in the US, Spanglish is what I speak. I don't speak Spanish like someone born and raised in Nicaragua. I don't speak English like someone born and raised in Boston, Georgia, or Wisconsin. Our speech reflects who we are and where we've been. My family is from Nicaragua; I was raised in LA; My grandparents speak Spanish; I went to English-only public schools in California; my friends speak English; my cousins speaks Spanglish, and so on and so forth.

"Una Muchachita" tries to identify what it means to be a Latina in the US. I wrote the poem in Spanglish because that's my language and the United States is my country. I'm not the only one. There are so many of us here in the US that speak Spanish, English, and Spanglish. But what does that mean? The poem tries to discover an answer and face the implications of speaking Spanglish in the US.

Questions

1.   What do you think about code-switching? Did you enjoy reading Spanglish and switching back and forth between English and Spanish? Why or why not?

2.   Do you speak Spanglish? Have you heard others in your family or community code-switch between English and Spanish?

3.   Why is the poem called "Una Muchachita"? What does being a girl have to do with how we speak?

4.   Why is Texas used in the poem as a symbol of the United States?

5.   What does the cockroach symbolize?

Writing Prompt

Whether or not you speak more than one language, let's write using more than one language! Write down ten nouns, names of people, places, and things. Translate these into Spanish using your own knowledge, Google Translate, or a bilingual dictionary. You should end up with a list of ten Spanish words.

Now, imagine you are walking down a street. All of a sudden a truck passes by with your name written on the side. What kind of a truck is this? What is being sold? Why is your name on the truck? What else is on the truck? Who is driving the truck? Where is it going? Answer these questions and follow your imagination. Just one thing—make sure to use your ten Spanish words.

Look it Up!

1.   Spanglish and code-switching

2.   Find two famous people from Texas. Extra points if these people are Latinos or Latinas!

3.   Mexican Texas and United States Texas. Did you know there are two?

Mujeres

Yo soy Adelita the third, the third
Adela in a backward line
of women before memory and photographs:
Mitadela or Tía Pinita rocking away
a hot afternoon in León, or it could be Managua.
I don't know. Todo se confunde.
It's not only me; we all contribute
to erasure: ¿Qué han hecho las mujeres,
las latinas, mejicanas, dominicanas,
puertorriqueñas, y si también las nicaragüenses?
Todas ocultadas in this US
culture, in this version of history.
To forget your mother's birthday
is to be una gran hija mala,
but of course I must take note
de todas esas mujeres de mi vida y del pasado.
Una después de otra contribuyendo,
haciendo, criando nuestras penas,
curando nuestras heridas, amándonos
por el resto de nuestras vidas.
I carry many names as daughter,
la hija de Juanita, Lela, Mitadela, y Tía Pinita.
A daughter de todas las planchadoras,
lavanderas, maestras y damas de casa
watching telenovelas on Univision wondering
if María Dolores will ever be found.
Does being a woman have to entail
una vida de sufrimiento?

I try to swing out from the shadows,
touch the lowest branch
of a eucalyptus tree, and over the years
have found words at rest in mi pasado y las voces
de las poetas olvidadas, the women, the mothers
alive in our hearts.
We look to the East
cada mañana y hambriente
para el sol
comienza la aurora.

Comment on "Mujeres"

Until I was seven years old, my mother made me wear dresses. I couldn't stand it! Then I found a pair of my brother's hand-me-down jeans, and that was it—I was a tomboy. Looking back on how I was raised, I chose to be a tomboy because it seemed that men and boys had all the power. I wanted some too! So for a while, I was tough and wore pants. I wouldn't let anyone get in my way. I thought power was tied to masculinity. But now, I'm know that's not true. Though men do have more access to powerful positions in society, such as being the head of businesses, colleges, and corporations, women have always had their own power. This "power" is sometimes difficult to see. The most energized aspect of being female is the power to give life. In Spanish, giving birth is dar luz—to bring to light. Women have the power to bring all of us to "light." Pretty amazing! This poem focuses on all the women that support, nurture, and bring us into this world.

Also since the poem is about women and written by a woman, the poem contributes to breaking down patriarchy and the conception that men are the most important gender. Reading and discussing this poem helps our society move toward a new understanding of what being male and female can mean. One of the responsibilities of a writer is that we can comment on society and through our words inspire others into a new understanding about our communities.

1. Why is the speaker of the poem confused at the poem's start?
2. Who are the important women in your life?
3. How have the women in your life contributed to your family?
4. What do you think about code-switching? Did you enjoy reading Spanglish and switching back and forth between English and Spanish? Why or why not?
5. The poem ends on an image of the coming dawn; what does daybreak symbolize?

Writing Prompt

Write about the women in your life. Make a list of all the women you know (at least five) and add a metaphor to describe them. If you prefer, simply focus on one woman and describe her using as many metaphors as possible. Use these metaphor frames to get started: My mother is a (choose an animal). My sister is a (choose a type of weather). My best friend is (choose a color). You can repeat the above metaphors by changing the animals, weather and colors. Also you can make metaphors by equating the women in your life to plants, food, cars, mystical creatures, scary creatures, keep going! Use your imagination. What are the women in your life like?

Look it Up!

1. Find one famous woman from a nation in Latin America.
2. What is Univision? If you know, what is their latest telenovela?
3. Are there any words you don't know in English or Spanish? Look it up!

Red Ants, Black Ants

An ant crawling through tattered books and files
hid under the shelf until I pinched it within
a thin white tissue. It didn't have wings, but
it could have been a termite preparing to bore
into wallboard and chew its way down
to the foundation. How strange

the way one ant on a wall next to a nail
comes forth unknown. A harbinger of why
I hate black ants and why Abuelita preserved
the red ones in mason jars. I have trouble
mixing the Wild West with Managua, Nicaragua
1908. Managua had to be green, but the poverty

and isolation of dry desert mesquite, beans
bubbling in an iron pot, fit stories
of hunger. Everyone. My grandmother stole
into the kitchen wearing a white
cotton frock embroidered with pineapples.
It could have been pale blue or yellow.

Definitely sleeveless in that humidity
and heat. Clear night skies are not frozen cold,
but a time when aunts, uncles, cousins and
grandmothers dream without sound.
Iguanas and monkeys. Huge cockroaches
with wings. In the night, a crescent moon would

have been enough for her to reach into a box lined
with wax paper. An iron box. A spicy hunk
of meat in her little scavenging hands
and the ants. The red ants biting her tongue.
Why do we love our families so much?
I had a hammer and nails. A piece of plywood.

I was determined to pound straight and true
under a Los Angeles sun and Abuelita's tomatoes,
five pearly bushes six feet tall. Green in arid
desert heat. From the garden hose, water
came out hot and splashed to dry dust. I sat
on clumps of grass, the board between my legs.

The nails wouldn't stay straight! They flopped
over as the hammer hit the head. It was hot.
I was sweaty, dirty and crying. Those damn
nails! And the ants crawling on my sneakers,
in my sock, up my leg! I'm sure she came out
and wiped me off, had me blow my nose,

and gave me a piece of pie. It wasn't pie.
It was torta. Out of a mix, but changed. An extra
egg. Whole milk. Los Angeles. Managua.
Verdant green mangroves and tile roofs.

Comment on "Red Ants, Black Ants"

I spent the summer when I was fourteen years old in Managua, Nicaragua. That was the one and only time I visited the country of my parent's birth. I've kept so many memories from that one month, a monkey on the roof, a school bus of boys yelling out of the window, but it hasn't been enough. I've always wondered what my life would have been like if I had been born in León, Chinandega, or Managua rather than San Francisco. "Red Ants, Black Ants" is a moment of trying to imagine the homeland. In the poem, I tie family stories about Nicaragua with me here in the United States. What crosses through time and history? Poems ride on the images they contain and many times, do double duty. On one level, an image should clearly convey the narrative and emotional trajectory of the poem. An image helps the reader to understand what is happening why, when, and to whom. In addition, images carry symbolic weight. They imply and mean more than their literal significance.

In this poem, there are many images that carry symbolic weight. The images relay what is happening, but what else is implied and carried within the poem's images? Think about the ants. Ants are literally little bugs. If a bunch of ants crawl on your leg that would be disgusting, and that is exactly what is happening in one part of the poem. But what else crawls around on our bodies? Memories, though not literally. There isn't a memory of my grandmother crawling on my leg, but memories stay with us. Memories about my grandmother are embodied in my heart, mind, and body, and so the ants are also symbolic of the memories I have about my grandmother.

Questions

1. What does the speaker of the poem see in the first stanza?
2. Think about the poem's title—why are ants important to the speaker?
3. What do you think about the world's little creatures, insects?
4. Where do your ancestor's come from? If you've been there, what was it like. If not, would you like to visit someday?
5. What do the ants literally do in the poem? What do they symbolize?

Writing Prompt

Write up a family story. What has someone in your family told you about their lives? Can you write down that story? Who is the person telling the story? What do you feel about them? When did the story take place? What happens to who? Why is this story important to you and your family?

Look it Up!

1. What is the wild, wild, West?
2. How did people preserve food before refrigeration?
3. When were refrigerators invented?

4:00 P.M. Watsonville

While I'm waiting for a signal light to change,
a gray metal tone rattles on the other side of the street.
A girl is bent over a bicycle.
Bare legs in knee-hi socks.
She walks toward double glass doors. Two trees.
Birds swivel under a telephone wire.
This is not important, but the birds were there.
I heard their noise. It stopped. I heard the trees.

Comment on "4:00 P.M. Watsonville"

When writing, I try to express feelings and ideas through images so that the reader can follow along by creating mental pictures. Hopefully, the reader will think about these mental pictures and begin to see how they go together or how they add a startling conflict to the poem.

In "4:00 P.M. Watsonville" a moment is captured. In this poem, one image moves to the next, and then the next. Everything moves and changes quickly, as it does in real life. Think about your day today. You woke up, did things, left the house, did things, went somewhere and did more things. When we break down our lives, so much happens in a moment. The poem is like a picture where time is stopped. It's the instant your finger clicks to capture the photo. Hopefully, you can join me outside and see the people, birds, and trees. The little things in life sometimes carry a great deal.

Questions
1.	What does the speaker of the poem see, feel, and hear?
2.	Where does the poem take place? A farm, a school, a city street? Why?
3.	What do you see when walking down the street?
4.	What mood is created at the poem's end?

Take a walk and notice. What do you see? What do you hear? What do you touch? What do you taste, or if you could, what would that taste like? What do you feel? Write exploring your senses. Make sure to describe what you see, hear, touch, taste, and feel. Can you discover a sixth sense? What would that be? Add that to your walk.

Look it Up!

1. What are the senses of the human body?
2. Why are the names of trees in your neighborhood?
3. What types of birds are in your neighborhood?

Early Morning Chat with God

This morning I'm back to asking for patience.
With my cup of coffee I sit outside to say hello
to you God, my Jiminy Cricket, my salsa
dancing quick-with-a-dip amigo. We have
a very collegial relationship. I laugh
at all your jokes and praise the wonders
of a sky's watercolors. I know you like me,
a benign affection and tolerance as I run
around like a chicken with its head cut off,
a gruesome image, nevertheless
hilarious like a grisly cartoon. The blood spurting.
The body winding down to zero. The crashing
into unforeseen objects. I think if I
were back on my great-grandmother's farm,
the farm that I know only through stories
my mother tells of Nicaragua, Bluefields,
a tortilla filled with just enough, and I saw
the long scrawny neck and the axe,
I would be sick to my stomach: the aimlessness
of the her final strut, the reality of blood
loss, her claws scratching the dirt, kicking up rocks,
a panic. But when she stops, into the pot
she goes. A meal, what we need to continue,
her flesh simmered off the bone. Delicious
in a tomato sauce flavored with green peppers
and onions. Transformation. The feathers
plucked, soil and dust washed away. The table set.
Goblets of red wine, white china plates,

a cast iron pot twirling a bay leaf
scented steam. Then a prayer and gratitude
that we have enough to make it through
another night alone, a night filled with longing
whispers and the turbulence of dreams.

Comment on "Early Morning Chat with God"

I love writing poetry particularly because I can leap from one idea to another. I can time travel too! In this poem, the speaker is in the United States and leaps back in time to Nicaragua and her great-grandmother's farm. Life is so complicated and poems try to catch that complexity by leaping back and forth from image to image, from idea to idea, and from time to time. Can you put it all together?

All throughout the American Southwest and in all countries of Latin America, missions, cathedrals, and churches are the center of cities and towns. The conquest of the Americas began with Spain and was tied directly to the Catholic Church. There is a strong connection between all peoples from Latin America and religion, particularly Catholicism. In this poem, the speaker addresses God as a friend, someone who brings joy to the world. But then the poem makes a leap into the speaker's feelings of separation from her family and other people. Poems leap from image to image since poems condense language and can contain many ideas. God, my family, my past are all tied together in the complexity of who I am and what I like to think about.

Questions
1.   Even though the poem is one long stanza, there are many leaps within its narrative; identify the various images, ideas, and time frames. How are they connected?
2.   What do you think about God? Do you ever talk to God or a higher power?

3.   Think about your ancestors; what type of life did your great-parents experience?

4.   The word, "transformation," is central to the poem; what is transformed in the poem?

Writing Prompt

Let's time travel. Imagine your great-grandparents. Both sets, one person, or any mix that you like. If you don't know who your great-grandparents are, guess. Bring them to life through your imagination. Where do they live? What type of work do they do? What year is it? What about relationships? Are they single, married, divorced, widowed? How old are they as you imagine their lives? Who do they love? What bothers them? What do they want most in the world? Time travel and visit your great-grandparents. What would you say, if you saw them?

Look it Up!

1.   The conquest and Catholicism
2.   Butchering a chicken
3.   Find a recipe for braised chicken that uses a bay leaf.

Chicanos in a Museum

And this time it was different.
Perla, Bilma, Clarissa, along with
Juvenal, two Alejandros, and un Ivan
walked into a palace of fine arts, a museum
of old depictions, depictions de la vida
y el coraje, paint on canvas, light reflected
pigments, an installation of a kitchen with posole
y los frijoles de tu mamá. They weren't seeking
job applications para trabajar toward
an American dream where they innocuously
wait to pick up paper towel trash
strewn across marble counters and floors,
and this time they weren't hidden
behind wallboard tinted hues
of indifference and invisibility.
They walked the halls; the halls
of a museum, el museo de Young, ese
museo de San Francisco. Respectability,
finance, approval of Chicano
art and its exhibit. Un special
que no estaba en K-Mart, pero allí
donde siempre estuvo: en el arte de la gente
los cuales fueron chavalitos
como estos camindo those hallways right
then and there. These kids didn't stare
at European landscapes choked by
industrial era smog beautified sunsets.
They didn't have to wonder why

bucolic cows rollick on rolling hills.
They didn't marvel at the silkiness tone
of fair white skin and embroidered
tapestry lace. Today esos Chicano
chavalitos, esos bilingual,
bicultural, Chicano, Mejicano, Latino,
Latina, American kids saw themselves,
not white, not wannabe white, but themselves
pintados y representado by those who
had come before. La familia, la Raza,
los antepasados reaching forward
and through to La Bilma, La Perla through paintings
on a wall, an electric fire connection.
Today los artistas, Chicano artists,
had a show, an entire exhibit, grants,
artist-in-residency titles, a whole show.
Three rooms, a band, and two lectures
para esos Chicanos, esos allí de las calles,
saliendo de esas mismas calles para pintar
nuestro futuro, that future where we all stand
looking up at the hills as they burn
a flame reaching toward the sun.

Comment on "Chicanos in a Museum"

I can still see Perla and Bilma learning how to silk screen with members from the Royal Chicano Airforce. Other artists sketch a portrait of Alejandro. There is a salsa band playing down the hall. A museum stores what a culture values. Through this exhibit, San Francisco expressed its value for the US Latino. We were in the halls and on the walls! In 2006, the de Young Museum of Fine Art in San Francisco hosted an exhibition of Chicano art, and I was grateful to visit the museum with a group of Puente Project students from Cabrillo College. Not only were there exhibits, but there were also hands-on art demonstrations and sessions. This day inspired a poem and stays in my mind since what we see in a museum can tell us who we are.

Over two hundred years ago, William Wordsworth in the *Preface to Lyrical Ballads* wrote that poetry should be written in everyday language in order to reach the most people. Poets have been thinking about this idea ever since. Currently, many Latinx poets write in Spanglish without italicization precisely because for Latinxs the mixture of English and Spanish is our everyday language. Also by using Spanglish we reach out to other Latinxs and call to mind the concept of being bilingual. For those who don't speak Spanglish, the poem is meant to call forth the complexity of languages used in the United States. The people of the United States have always spoken various languages, even before there was a United States. Our linguistic history is indeed vast.

Questions

1.   What type of art is on display in this museum? How do you know?

2.   The poem ends with the hills burning—what can this symbolize about the future for our nation?

3.   Have you ever been to a museum? If so, what happened that day? If not, is there a local museum you can visit?

4.   Why is art important in our lives as individuals and as a culture?

Writing Prompt

An ekphrastic poem is a poem inspired by a work of art. Find any painting created by a Latinx artist and write an ekphrastic poem. If you need help getting started, look at the painting and come up with one word that captures the painting's mood. Use that word at the beginning of each line and write at least seven lines. You can describe the colors in the poem, the objects depicted, how the lines of the painting move, and anything else you notice. You can state what the chosen word means to you, means to a friend or means to a family member. You can state the opposite of the chosen word. Keep writing until you feel the poem is "finished."

Look it Up!

1.   Who is William Wordsworth?

2.   What was shown in the Chicano Art Exhibit at the de Young Museum in 2006?

3.   Research Chicano Art; can you name three Chicano artists?

31

San Francisco

My great-grandmother taught my mother to read using chalk
and a black slate in León where adobe brick
buildings are white-washed Spaniards

and history. We brought with us red and blue macaws, panthers,
and crocodiles. Tooling up and down
Dolores Street hills, my Papi rode

a bicycle delivering Lela's nacatamales. Back and forth
from a clock tower at the end of Market Street,
a renovated 1919 streetcar,

transplanted from Milan, works tourist dollars. Advertisements
from the late sixties posted behind
True View Plexiglass. I can't read a word

of the Italian glitz, nor fathom the deep blue of the Mediterranean
while sipping an ice cold Coca-Cola, but there is a warm blanket
on a wooden bench and a leather

hand hook. Above a Cuban restaurant, where waiters serve
black bean hummus and chocolate croissants,
hangs the gay pride flag alongside

a Direct TV satellite dish. Gabby walks to school, Pokémon
cards in his pocket. Sanchez Street. I work
in the kitchen with my Lela. Mariposa Avenue,

Valencia Street, Camino Real, are added to masa. Homemade
        tortillas puff into sweetness. I'm not
                one third Irish, one half German

and two parts English with a little Cherokee thrown in,
        but last night I couldn't translate the word "hinge"
                on every door that opens and closes

to clouds beyond four walls. An old lady, perhaps Cambodian,
        Vietnamese, Korean, something of her own,
                hurries off the 31 Stockton while

my Tía Teresa double parks in front of the mercados on 24th Street
        para los quesos y los chiles in the backroom. One
                whiff and the world is not so small.

Comment on "San Francisco"

Sometimes, I like to imagine that we leave a part of ourselves everywhere we go. If we could travel back in time, my father would be on a bike delivering nacatamales because he really did that. My mother would be learning to write in León. I would be on a street car and notice someone's forgotten woolen scarf. Our lives are made of details, and so are poems. Many times, a detail in a poem is called an image. And many times, an image is linked to a memory. Poems collect memories. The memories a writer places into a poem can connect to those of the reader. Writing then becomes about connection. We can reach out to each other by reading and writing, even though centuries pass. This poem is direct autobiography. I was born in San Francisco, and we lived there until I was five years old. Even though we moved, I kept going back because my extended family lived in the city. I have this city engraved in my memories. What I've done here is to weave together my experience with that of my mother, father, aunts, uncles, and there is even a great-grandmother in the poem.

Questions

1. The poem is titled, "San Francisco," so what is this city like according to the poem?
2. Have you ever been to San Francisco or live there? If so, what did you see? If not, what cities have you visited?
3. How does the poem change from where it starts to where it ends?
4. Identify three images in the poem. What memories do these hold?

34

<u>Writing Prompt</u>

Let's remember! Memories stick in our minds because something important, interesting, or confusing happened. Think of a memory. Allow one to pop into your mind. How old are you? What are you doing? What are you wearing? Who is with you? Where are you? What do you feel? What are the people around you doing? If you could re-enter this memory what would you do?

<u>Look it Up!</u>
1.   San Francisco
2.   What is a nacatamale?
3.   What type of businesses are there on 24th Street in San Francisco?

Conversation with Rubén Darío's "Eco y yo"

Rubén, el gran poeta de Nicaragua,
in the sadness of his childhood
my father knew you.

He learned to love art
and how to weave a grand old narrative
with a grade school education
bought by sweaty dollars
sent from los Estados Unidos
by my grandmother.

He believes that poetry is something special, something worthy,
something his daughter is allowed to do,

though he would prefer I write
song lyrics for the next breakthrough
Latin hit on the U.S. pop charts.

Señor Darío, though you're long dead and buried
in the city of León where you were baptized
and a stone lion weeps over your tomb,
I call you back,
my elitist fatman, to play
poetry's muse
draped in garlands and white chiffon.

*

Las obras suyas, your poetry, offers thick oaken doors on a
Moorish palace,

a unicorn, and a swan. And I attempt to follow

your technique for rhyme, how you lay down
streets paved gold, how through language

we rise to a palatial state of mind.

But in following a palace,
I arrive at fallace, fallacy

as if it's all a lie.
How nothing is ever enough.

How it all can go

from you Rubén,
you, your mansion and your swans.

*

Rubén, I believe in all that is beautiful,
but I could never be a dove.

All I know are pigeons on Market Street,
right outside Burger King,
two blocks up from City Hall.

Show me how to navigate sadness, sail through

every emotion and its incantation
spray-painted on cinderblock walls.

I haven't been able to avoid the dream

for all that is bright and cheerful. I can't
let go those three seconds

one summer day when the sun hit
the sea and there was nothing
more than clear blue.

And blue is the sky, and blue is time, and blue stands still
while we wait

because there is no other choice.

Your gypsy has packed up her tarot cards,
star charts, and dice.
She has thrown her bags
into the back of a two-tone rusted pick-up
and is heading on out of town.

*

La patria, the homeland, the soil.
So many have left.

In Managua, when my father failed
fifth grade and altered his report card,
no-one noticed.

He never forgave his aunt
for making him an errand boy
instead of a nephew,
for making him run
to the grocers, to the pharmacy,
until he ran here to the States

back to his mother, my grandmother,
my Lela, after whom I am named.

Here the supermarkets
are so big we should be ashamed
of all our demands and desires.
Each time I'm at Safeway, Hardings, D&W,
I check out mangoes
mostly green, mostly not ready yet.

And I can be nothing but
the mix of here and there, not one
not the other. Not Nica.

Not gringa.

Mezcla. Mestizaje.

Los dos fit better than one alone.

*

You, Rubén, left behind a tapestry

sewn with gilded thread: your ornate
and elaborate poems that I found
in a Spanish language bookstore
off Valencia Street
in San Francisco where I am
the vowels, syllables, the names
of streets. Los nombres de la calle . . .

mas me libró en toda parte
        arte

That's your line Rubén and your belief
that art metaphorically breaks
the binds that strap us into ourselves,

but more so the ability
        to imagine,

the ability to conjure up hope
out of nowhere, nothing,
        and face off despair.

Irises, orchids, tiger lilies dance

in air from where we have come
to where we must go.

The void
can be obscured by a rose or a pair
of glasses tinted blue.

So, let death take her sour bite.

Out of the delirium,
the sweat, the anxiety of every morning,
we weave a soft and tender sea,

the mermaids, the song,

the possibility,

and all begins again.

Comment on "Conversation with Rubén Darío's 'Eco y yo'"

Poetry runs in my cultural DNA. My mother relates stories about going to the theater, not to see a play, but to listen to famous actresses recite poetry. Once I went to an Easter brunch at my great-aunt's house, and we all gathered around to listen to one of the guests recite poetry. In Nicaragua, poetry is it. I didn't know this until I started reading and realized the truth about my own poetic heritage. In addition, I discovered Rubén Darío. He is a world renown poet who heralds the movement in Spanish poetry called Modernismo. So this poem begins as an imagined conversation with this impressive man of my poeticimagination and heritage.

One idea that inspires every poet is Ezra Pound's notion to "make it new." In order to make it new, a poet needs to read everything so that they know what has been written before. As a Latina writer that means I have to read US poets and poets from Latin America. I have a double duty or a double opportunity. So "Conversation" arose from an imagined discussion I had with Darío. Due to time, language, and the fact that I'm not in Nicaragua, my experience is vastly different from Darío's, and the poem explores all those complexities.

The poem is a long one, but I hope you're up to the challenge. Each section is an interaction with the ideas in Darío's work and my experience here in the United States. The poem moves from Nicaragua to the US in its topics, language, and stories. I hope you find Dario's blue tinted glasses and mermaids as captivating as I have.

Questions
1.   The poem is written in sections; outline the major ideas in each section. Look at these ideas and put them together; what is the poem's central premise about living in the United States as a Latinx?
2.   "Los dos fit better than one alone" holds the poems contradictions; what are these things that are better together? Come up with all the ways that duality is a strength.
3.   Is there a famous person from your heritage that you find inspiring? What is their story? If you don't know, then look it up!
4.   Darío's work focuses on the power of the imagination; if you could imagine a better world, what would that look like?

Writing Prompt
Find a famous person from your heritage and have a conversation with them. First you'll need to find someone, and Wikipedia is the place to go. Look up the country, and you'll find the names of important people in that nation's history. Keep clicking until you've gotten enough information about that person, then talk back! Why is this person's story interesting to you? What do you want to know about their life? What would you ask them if you could call them up? Speak your mind. Tell them about how life is today.

<u>Look it Up!</u>

1.   Who is Rubén Darío?
2.   What is a Moorish place?
3.   Find a picture of Darío's tomb.

Idiomas Desconocidas

The scar of the mountain is as beautiful as the mountain.
The withered branch of the tree bends gracefully to tierra.
Desert earth puts forth one miniature orange flower.
There is softness in the green broken burr.
And still what captures most are leaves lifting
as wind sopla en idiomas desconocidas.

Comment on "Idiomas Desconocidas"

The poem's title roughly translates to "unknown languages," but this poem only has three Spanish words, so it isn't necessarily about speaking Spanish or English. Language is about communication, and in order to communicate there always has to be an "other," a mother, a brother, someone at school, someone we're reading, someone to send a text to. Originally as babies we learn language by listening to our mothers as they hush us to sleep or by listening to the neighbors on a summer afternoon. Even when we're alone, we are talking to ourselves, to our inner self. There is always an engagement of two parts. But what about all that is around us? Do plants, animals, insects, mountains communicate? What do they send out to the world? What do we pick up? Is there more than just people talking and texting? The unknown languages in this poem are those of the world around, the mountain, tree, and desert. As a bilingual Latina, I live with contradictions: I can see how the beauty of the mountain expands through its scar. All around, the world keeps trying to tell us something. We just need to notice.

Questions

1. Do the images in the poem evoke a positive or negative tone?
2. What languages are present in the poem?
3. How has the natural world communicated with you?
4. If you could visit one natural location of spectacular beauty, where would that be?
5. Can a cell phone be beautiful?

Writing Prompt

Think about an outdoor location that you have visited. This could be the neighborhood park, a national forest, the seashore, driving up to the mountains, driving through agricultural fields. Pick one location. Make a list of nouns found in that place, and try to include large items, such as the sky, and small items, such as ants. Arrange the nouns from largest to smallest or smallest to largest. Write a sentence for each in the order you've chosen.

Look it Up!

1.   Where is the nearest state park in your area and what can you do there?
2.   Discover the names of three trees in your neighborhood, school, or city.
3.   Is there life on Mars?

Lorca's Rain

No te puedo decir. Sometimes,
I lose the words. El caracol
came from the onion skin pages
of Lorca's collected works.
A book found in a dresser drawer
alongside sticky Polaroid photos,
receipts from the cleaners, and
a bottle of aspirin. My mother
brought his poems from Nicaragua,
along with a language woven
through memory and distance.
Now I speak Spanglish under
a wet sky, while orange poppies
lie low holding the weight of water.
Los caracoles in my garden grow
fat from rain and are eating away
an unidentified citrus; will it turn
out to be an orange or a lemon tree?
And the succulent jade. The leaves
all caracoled out. Snail bitten to pieces.
Where do they hide their teeth?
Then the rain. On Sunday.
Forgiven again. Water can cleanse,
dissolve mud stained smears,
and cast away what we do
to ourselves, those mistakes
we fold past in order to move on.
The poppies should dry out.

Los caracoles will continue to grow.
I have always loved my mother.
Even when language is not,
when doubt commands a heavy sky,
when a breath is hard to come by,
I will put down words dressed in red,
y palabras hechas para atras.

Comment on "Lorca's Rain"

Have you ever snuck into your parent's bedroom and looked in the drawers? I did. Lots of times. Once I found a book by Federico Garcia Lorca that my mother had brought from Nicaragua and which she had kept over the years. What amazed me was that my mother had packed her clothes, shoes, and everything else she would need in a new country, and she also packed a book of poems, plays, stories, and essays. That book had to be important.

By the time I found that book, my mother had been in the States nearly twenty years. So not only did she bring it with her, she took care of it over and over, after my brother was born, after I was born, after we moved from San Francisco to LA. Without saying a word that book spoke to me about how important my mother's language was to her, and so to me too. Also that book was more than just pages, it was her culture, the poems, the stories, how Nicaragua and Spain are intertwined. There is so much in our pasts that deserve to arrive in the present and to be kept strong. It is by our connections backwards that we realize all that has led up to our own lives. It's important to turn around and look.

Questions
1.   At the beginning of the poem, why can't the speaker of the poem find the correct words?
2.   Why does the speaker of the poem look in her mother's dresser drawer? What is she curious about discovering?

3.   What does the speaker of the poem discover in her mother's dresser drawer and what do these things tell her about herself and her mother?

4.   Have you ever looked through your parents personal items? If so, what did you find?

Writing Prompt

Find an object in your home that has belonged to your parents, grandparents, or some other member of your family. (If you can't find that, then pick any object that you have in your house.) Describe the object: what is it? What colors? What size? What does it feel like when held? Is it beautiful, ugly, somewhere between? Who has used this object? Is it always used for what it is meant for? What has this object seen? What has this object heard?

Look it Up!

1.   Have you discovered Google translate? What is a caracol?

2.   Who is Federico Garcia Lorca?

3.   What are polaroid photos?

To My Childrens

I call you "Hon" for honey, honey bee, be my honey.

After each flower, fly home. Wrapped in football,
geometry and various shades of skin: caramel, chocolate,

vanilla hazelnut. Fly home with a deep cinnamon tan
though I will always know
there's a vanilla pudding belly under that shirt!

My childrens. ¡La gran mestizaje de las Americas!

But be more than careful. The world expects
you to get in trouble. A brick smashed
window. A chocolate bar slid into a pocket.
Copying answers on that test.
          Don't do it.

The big "there." The big "them." Whiteness. Power. Societal
structures of post-racial America where "they" are blinded
by a snow storm of reasons why not,
not in my neighborhood.

All wait for you to fail. It's expected for you

to kick Romeo and Juliet across the parking lot. No-one will
notice

as you stare out the window when the teacher

annotates the connection between metaphors and reality.
D's are passing grades.
A girl is a biaaaatch and gold grillz glisten celebrity status.

Don't do it.

You are expected to end up in jail, divorced, homeless,
unemployed, raging and violent. Not understanding why.

You had to read Malcom X to discover your own vitality.
Jesus isn't a white man with blue eyes. You're not supposed to
know

that covered wagons were stealth bombers setting off genocide.
That before corporations rolled over family farms,
those families "removed" Cherokee,
Shawnee, the mothers, the fathers, the children,

my children, our children.

The childrens of brown cinnamon warm spice
have danced on shotgun shells, bowie knives, and shards of
glass.
You are supposed to drop out of high school and never go to
college.
Never read Fredrick Douglass or Eduardo Galeano.
Don't take that sociology class. History is boring.
God is dead. Religion an opiate. Get a job. Go to work.

Don't you want that nice black muscle car with silver gray lining
and midnight rims?

Don't do it. Graduate. Go to college.

My childrens. The godhead grows
from palm fronds, deep night stars,
waves of heat and humidity
wrapped round the equator.

We are all divine.

My childrens. You have a responsibility to rise above
inundating waves of indifference and invisibility.
>Stand up.
>Be seen.
>Listen to your own voice. You are right.

The world is not fair. You are not privileged.
>But you are strong.
Raise your hand.
Open a book.

>Rise.

>Discover
you are elemental,
a comet raised from stardust.
Shoot
through night time sky.
Spiral
through the universe.

Comment on "To My Childrens"

Did you notice how the title uses "childrens" instead of "children"? I did that on purpose to show that this poem is for children of color, my children, my childrens. I have two boys who sometimes get in trouble, and part of being a parent is to worry. As a person of color, there is an additional worry. I fear that all the negative messages about being shades of brown will end up etched on my children's bodies. I worry that all these messages will lead my children to believe that they are less than stardust. And by children I don't mean just my two boys, but all of you. My childrens. So the poem.

Discussions about race and racism are continuous and never ending. There is no point where to stop. Conversations about what it means to grow up in the United States as a person of color, Latinx, Black, Asian, East Asian, Pacific Islander, and all the other shades of brown, are complex and difficult. Hopefully, this poem leads people to think about the pitfalls out there and serves to remind about the beauty and power within every human being. It is true. We are made of stardust. The science behind that claim is that the building blocks of life came to this planet on comets that crashed. After every explosion, the dust settles and life continues.

Questions
1.   What does the poem warn against? What are you not supposed to do?
2.   What does the poem suggest that children do? Why?

3.   The poem ends with an image of a comet—what does this image symbolize?

4.   Where are you at this moment? How can you live up to your heritage as stardust?

5.   What is your most difficult struggle?

Writing Prompt

Sometimes we feel before we can articulate ideas and points of view. What do you feel about your heritage? First, who are your parents and what have they given you? Keep going backwards. Who are your grandparents and what have they given you? Keep going backwards. Who are your great-grandparents and what have they given you? Keep going backwards. You may not know who the specific people are, but you can generalize. What part of the world is your family from? What type of work did they do there? Were they farmers, ranchers, doctors, lawyers, blacksmiths, housewives, etc? What values do they have and pass down? Did they value hard work, honesty, taking risks, keeping the family together, celebrating holidays, going to church, etc. What do you feel about yourself and your ancestors? Go ahead: be confused, angry, joyful, proud . . .connect yourself to those who have come before.

Look it Up!

1.   What is the science behind comets seeding life on Earth?

2.   Who is Fredrick Douglass?

3.   Who is Eduardo Galeano?

Acknowledgements

Many thanks to Maria Maloney at Mouthfeel Press and Rubie Grayson at Unsolicited Press where many of these poems first appeared in book form.

From *Split Geography*, Mouthfeel Press:
"4:00 P.M. Watsonville" as "4:00 P.M. Kalamazoo"
"Chicanos in a Museum"
"Una Muchachita"

From *Twice Told Over*, Unsolicited Press:
"Conversation with Rubén Darío's 'Eco y yo'"
"Early Morning Chat with God"
"Lorca's Rain"
"Red Ants, Black Ants"
"San Francisco"
"San Martín de Porres"
Also thanks to the following journals for publishing some of the poems in this collection:
"An Ambiguity." Bordersenses
"Mujeres." Porter Gulch Review

Finally, thanks to the Puente Project, Cabrillo College, my family and friends for supporting this work throughout the years.

65982194R00042

Made in the USA
Middletown, DE
06 March 2018